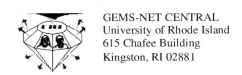

GEMS-NET CENTRAL
University of Rhode Island
615 Chafee Building
Kingston, RI 02881

W9-DII-377

HISTORY OF WOMEN IN SCIENCE FOR YOUNG PEOPLE

Written and Illustrated by
Vivian Sheldon Epstein

ACKNOWLEDGEMENTS

I am grateful to the authors of books geared to adults about women involved in science.

I am indebted to my husband, Ted Epstein, Jr., for his suggestions and constant encouragement of any endeavor I undertake. Our world needs more encouraging men.

The following people gave me their time, expertise, and suggestions for which I am most thankful:

Brenda Sheldon	Editorial suggestions
Elizabeth Epstein	Computer consultant
Pam Sandlian	Denver Public Library Children's Library Manager
Judy C. Curtis	Curriculum Specialist for Denver Public Schools Science Education, Mathematics, and Health
Jane S. Day	Ph.D. Archaeology, Chief Curator of the Denver Museum of Natural History
Martin M. Maltempo	Professor and Chair Department of Physics University of Colorado at Denver
Clyde Zaidins	Professor of Physics, Astrophysics Researcher in Nuclear Physics University of Colorado at Denver
Susan Avery	Ph.D. Atmospheric Physics, University of Colorado
Eric Snyder	Department of Molecular Cellular Biology and Developmental Biology University of Colorado
Jeremy A. Lazarus	Psychiatrist, Denver, Colorado
Jane M. Comstock	Senior Instructor in Art History Department of Fine Arts University of Colorado at Denver
Julie A. Johnson	Ph.D. Zoology, Executive Administrator Center for Tropical Conservation Duke University, Durham, North Carolina

INTRODUCTION

People have always tried to understand their world. Primitive people explained the mysteries of life and death, day and night, and all they saw by thinking the "gods" were the cause of these actions. Myths began. Some people in each society looked at life a little differently. They observed carefully, gathered information and had creative ideas. They tested their creative ideas many times until they knew they worked. The ideas then might remain useful or become helpful inventions. These people became the first scientists.

A SCIENTIST is a person who:

looks for clues to explain our world,
wants to understand how things work,
stubbornly keeps an idea which others think wrong,
patiently tests the idea many times to see if it truly works,
and relies on evidence from many observations,
not on preconcieved ideas.

As society became more complex, people formed schools to learn the facts of our world. It was thought that formal education for women was not necessary. They were not allowed to enter schools or universities. If a woman could not share in book knowledge and exchange ideas, it was difficult for her to be a scientist, even though she had many creative ideas. There were women in each century who had great intelligence and determination to be better educated and to become scientists. These women paved the way for others and created wonderful role models.

Women are half of the human species, but have often been excluded. Rosalyn Yalow, the 1977 Nobel Prize winner, said "The world cannot afford the loss of talents of half of its people if we are to solve the many problems which beset us."

TABLE OF CONTENTS

There is much overlap in the contributions of these women from one category to another, but to help identify their actions the following divisions are created:

By studying simple societies of today and finding tools that were buried in the earth long ago, good guesses can be made of how people lived before history was written in books. Thousands of years ago, women and men each did special work to help the people of their group. Women gathered food to share with others. Women became inventors when they created baskets of grass and pots of clay in order to carry more food and water. Through gathering, women learned about plants and noticed that some herbs and plants could make sick people feel better. Women became healers.

In much later societies of Egypt, Greece, and Rome, people remembered what women had done by creating myths or stories of women as goddesses. Many female goddesses of medicine were worshipped, some named Hygeia, Panacea, Astarte, Isis, and Artemis. Maybe in the very earliest groups of people women and men worked together equally. Sadly, when civilizations became more complex, women and their work were less valued. Women were usually not allowed to have education or power in public. There were some exceptions.

HYPATIA (Rome, Alexandria, Egypt, 370-415)

Hypatia was considered the most well-known female scientist until Marie Curie.

Hypatia's father wanted his daughter to have what many other Roman women at the time were not given, a fine education. From her tutors, she learned and quickly mastered mathematics, astronomy and natural science. Because of her brilliant mind, she was appointed head of the University of Alexandria where she taught mathematics and philosophy. Hypatia wrote thirteen books about arithmetic and algebra. She designed several scientific instruments. She gave lectures about the values of the early Greek philosophers, their respect for science and their better treatment of women. Many people listened to Hypatia, and she became an advisor to the government. Hypatia lived at the time when Christianity was growing and the Roman Empire was ending. Her teachings and writings angered Cyril, the new Christian ruler of Alexandria. On his orders, Hypatia was very cruelly murdered and later all her writings were burned. Almost all respect for science and questioning had ended. The Dark Ages had begun.

During the Dark Ages, questioning and a scientific view of life was not encouraged by the Christian rulers of western society. Most people could not read or write. Between the sixth and eleventh centuries, the only place where women could get an education was the convent.

HILDEGARD OF BINGEN (Germany, 1098-1179)

Hildegard was the first woman scientist whose writings still exist.

Hildegard was the tenth child born to a wealthy German family. One of the few places a woman could receive a formal education was in a convent or abbey where Christian nuns lived, worked and taught. From the age of eight, Hildegard lived in a small convent where she learned Latin, the Scriptures and music. Hildegard was like some other women of her day who chose convent life rather than marriage. Most of these women came from the upper classes or royalty, as convents asked for a large dowry (money and material goods) to "marry Christ." Hildegard became an abbess, the leader of the abbey of religious women. In addition to traveling, teaching medicine and religion, Hildegard had religious visions which she spoke about to many people, including the Pope. She wrote an encyclopedia of natural history as well as a medical book describing causes and cures of illness. Hildegard was the first author who wrote about the need to boil drinking water. She taught the importance of cleanliness and diet, exercise and rest. Hildegard of Bingen was a powerful woman who had many roles: abbess, scientist, medical expert and author of medical books, and composer of music. She was influential in politics and religion.

By the 13th century, a very few women, especially in Italy, were being educated in the growing cities. The women interested in science were either wealthy noblewomen or had fathers who had taught them a craft such as painting.

MARIA SIBYLLA MERIAN (Germany, 1647-1717)

Maria Sibylla Merian combined her talent in art with her interest in science. She created paintings and wrote books about plants and insects that were used by scientists for study.

Maria Sibylla Merian, Illustration from DISSERTATION IN INSECT GENERATIONS AND METAMORPHOSIS IN SURINAM. Bound volume of 72 hand-colored engravings, 2nd edition. (1719). "Gift of Wallace and Wilhelmina Holladay." The National Museum of Women in the Arts.

As a child in Germany, Maria loved to study and collect insects. Her stepfather, a flower and insect painter, encouraged Maria and taught her about painting. Maria then created watercolor and oil pictures of birds and insects, such as spiders, caterpillars, and ants. As a young woman, she wrote several books about insects. Her illustrations were so accurate they were used by scientists. After twenty years of marriage, adventurous Maria divorced her husband and traveled to South America with one of her two daughters. She was 52 years old. They lived in the jungle of Surinam where Maria painted birds, insects and flowers. She was interested in the life cycles of insects, observing them carefully, and then drawing their development. When she returned to Europe she lived in Amsterdam, Holland, where her illustrations about the growth of each insect became a popular book, purchased by individuals and libraries. Maria created beautiful illustrations of plants never before seen by people of Western Europe. Six plants, nine butterflies, and two beetles are named for Maria Sibylla Merian. She was able to use her talents as an artist to teach about the study of insects, which is the science of entomology.

Modern astronomy began in the late 16th and early 17th centuries with the invention of the telescope. In Germany, some women became astronomers and worked as helpers to their fathers, brothers, or husbands. In the United States in the 19th century, one woman who was an astronomer carried on this tradition and made her own discovery.

MARIA MITCHELL (U.S.A., 1818-1889)

Maria Mitchell discovered a comet and was the first professor of astronomy at Vassar College.

Maria's family could not afford to send her to any of the very few universities that accepted women, but her job as a librarian gave her the chance to get a good education by reading books on many subjects. Maria was talented in mathematics and always helped her father, an astronomer, measure the position of the stars. She had so closely observed the skies through a telescope that she was aware of the smallest changes in groups of stars. Suddenly, on October 1, 1847, Maria Mitchell noticed a white spot that had not been in the skies before, carefully wrote down the figures, and knew she had discovered a comet never before seen by anyone else. Maria became famous and traveled to Europe to meet other scientists and royalty. She felt lucky to have had a father who believed that she had to use her mind. Matthew Vassar also believed in Maria, asking her to become professor of astronomy at the first college for women which he founded, Vassar College. Maria taught and continued to observe the skies. She was the first person in the United States to photograph the sun's surface. Maria Mitchell wrote articles, gave lectures, and encouraged women to seek more education.

FLORENCE NIGHTINGALE (England, 1820-1910)

Florence Nightingale was the pioneer of the modern nursing profession.

In the 1800s, hospitals in England were overcrowded and dirty; diseases spread easily. There were no trained nurses. Florence wanted to help the sick and poor people in hospitals. Even though her wealthy parents were very much against the idea, Florence went to Germany to learn about nursing. During the Crimean War, Florence was put in charge of all hospitals in the war zone. The wounded English soldiers had little water and were in filthy buildings with no medical equipment. Florence trained thirty-eight nurses, found some medical supplies, had hospital rooms cleaned and painted and bed sheets washed, hired a chef to make healthy food, wrote patient reports and set up reading, writing, and game areas. She greatly improved the quality of care given to the soldiers. When she returned to England, she opened the Nightingale School and Home for Nurses. Because of her influence, hard work, and the hundreds of letters she wrote, Florence Nightingale helped improve hospitals and patient care in England and India. She wrote a book on better hospital design and one about nursing care, stressing the need for cleanliness, order and sensitivity to patients' feelings. Florence Nightingale raised the importance of nursing by teaching that good patient care can save lives.

CLARA BARTON (U.S.A., 1821-1912)

Clara Barton was the founder of the American Red Cross.

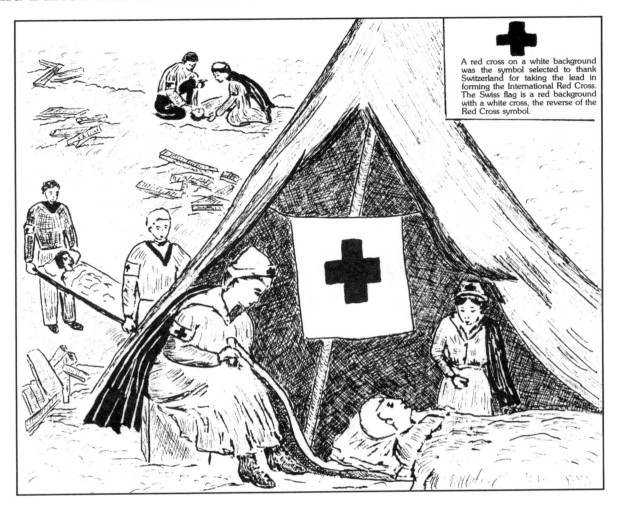

A red cross on a white background was the symbol selected to thank Switzerland for taking the lead in forming the International Red Cross. The Swiss flag is a red background with a white cross, the reverse of the Red Cross symbol.

As a shy and caring child, Clara nursed her sick brother to health. For many years she was a school teacher. In 1861, when the U.S. Civil War began, Clara saw that wounded soldiers were without food, water or medical supplies while waiting to be taken to hospitals. Using her own initiative, Clara placed a newspaper ad to get donated supplies. In the middle of battle, she bravely distributed the items by mule team to the grateful men, and nursed them until the end of the war. She became ill from overwork and went to Europe for a rest. There she heard about the International Committee of the Red Cross which helped care for the wounded on both sides during wartime. For <u>five</u> years Clara Barton tried to convince people that the United States should join this humanitarian group. She overcame her shyness and courageously spoke on behalf of others. In 1882 she succeeded; the American Red Cross was organized and Clara Barton became its first president. She expanded the services of the American Red Cross for the next 23 years while also helping people in world-wide disasters during peacetime. Clara wrote books about her experiences and those of the Red Cross. Clara Barton greatly helped reduce human suffering through her caring, hard work and vision in founding the American Red Cross.

For thousands of years of pre-history and in the ancient civilizations of Sumeria, Greece and Egypt, women helped heal others. In the second century of the Roman Empire, there were some notable women doctors specializing in female health care. In the eleventh century, the earliest medical school was founded in Salerno, Italy, with women professors on its faculty. In later centuries, women were no longer allowed in European medical schools. The first American medical school began in 1767 at the University of Pennsylvania; they did not allow women as students.

ELIZABETH BLACKWELL (England, U.S.A., 1821-1910)

Elizabeth Blackwell was the first woman doctor in the U.S.A. She opened a hospital with only women doctors on the staff and started a medical school for women, paving the way for many other women to become doctors.

Elizabeth wanted to do something no other woman in the United States had ever done: become a doctor. Growing up in a family that believed girls and boys should have equal education, she soon found out that others did not share this idea. No medical school in the U.S. would accept her simply because she was a woman. The professors of Geneva Medical College in New York also did not want to accept a woman, but allowed the students to decide. The male students, as a joke, voted yes, and Elizabeth became the first woman to enter medical school. Even though she graduated at the top of her class, Geneva Medical College refused all other women students. Because no hospital in the U.S. would allow Elizabeth the chance to intern (practice), she took this extra training in France. There she became blind in one eye, infected by one of her patients. When she returned to the U.S., she found that patients were not willing to come to a woman doctor. Not accepted by society, Elizabeth was sad and lonely. She chose not to marry, but later happily adopted a daughter. Elizabeth's sister, Emily, became a doctor and they opened a hospital staffed only by women doctors. Dr. Elizabeth Blackwell then started a medical school for women, training hundreds to become doctors.

MYRA ADELE LOGAN (U.S.A., 1908-1977)

Dr. Myra Adele Logan was the first woman surgeon to operate on the human heart.

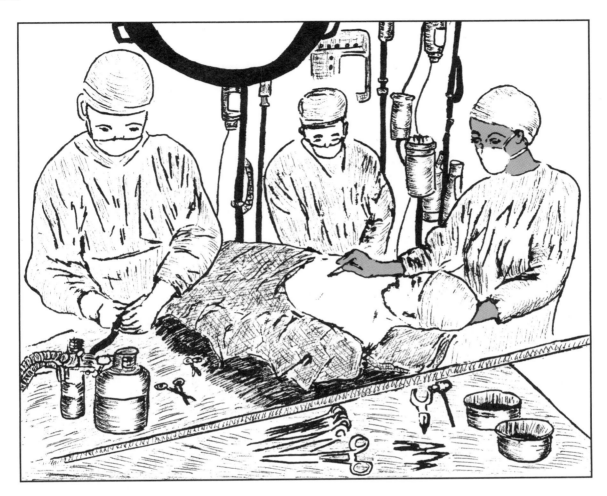

Myra's mother was unusual as she had attended Atlanta University at a time when most women did not go to college. Myra's father was trustee and treasurer of a college, Tuskegee Institute. From her parents Myra learned to value education and received top honors in school. Myra wanted to become a doctor and won the Walter Gray Crump Scholarship for Black Women. After medical school, all doctors must have more practice called internship and residency, which Myra did by performing surgery in the emergency room of New York City's Harlem Hospital. Dr. Myra Logan then became one of the first surgeons and the first woman surgeon to operate on the human heart. She also repaired other parts of the human body, did research on helpful drugs, wrote many professional reports and spoke to large groups of doctors about her findings. Dr. Logan's work was so well respected that she was invited to join an exclusive group, the American College of Surgeons, and became its first black woman member. Dr. Myra Adele Logan worked with the New York State Fair Employment Practices Committee and the National Association for the Advancement of Colored People. Her goal was to help people of different races better understand each other without making judgements by the color of one's skin.

ANTONIA COELLO NOVELLO (Puerto Rico, U.S.A., 1944 -)

Dr. Antonia Coello Novello became the first Hispanic and the first female surgeon general of the United States.

Until the age of eighteen, Antonia needed yearly hospital treatment. After finally having surgery to correct the problem, Antonia vowed to become a doctor to help others. Her father died when she was young; her mother, a school principal, encouraged Antonia's dream. Antonia went to medical school at the University of Puerto Rico, had further training in public health, and learned more about the illnesses of children, called pediatrics. She developed a private practice, and because she was an expert in both child care and public health, Dr. Novello was asked to become deputy director of the National Institute of Child Health and Human Development. In 1990, George Bush, President of the United States, appointed Dr. Antonia Coello Novello to be Surgeon General of the United States. Dr. Novello became the first woman and first Hispanic in this position of highest ranking doctor of the U.S. government. She encouraged people to be responsible for their own bodies, stressing the dangers of alcohol and smoking. She wanted better AIDS education and improved health care for minorities, women and children. Using her position in government, Dr. Antonia Coello Novello spoke up for people who were not able to speak for themselves.

MARGARET SANGER (U.S.A., 1879-1966)

Margaret Sanger helped women learn to control their own bodies and decide whether and when to have children. She called this "birth control."
It is still difficult today for women in many parts of the world to find out about birth control.

Margaret Sanger was born the sixth of eleven children. She became a nurse, visiting people in their homes. She noticed that poor people had many more children than wealthy people. Parents loved their children, wanting to give each child attention and material goods, but having many children often made this very difficult. Mothers begged Margaret Sanger to teach them how to space their pregnancies. With her husband and three children, Margaret sold their home, took their savings, and went to the doctors of Europe to find answers. She learned how to help women control their pregnancies, which she called "birth control." She wrote about birth control and opened information clinics to help women plan the size of their families. This was against the law and Margaret was arrested and jailed many times. Margaret tried to change the law. She became a public speaker, wrote books, mailed thousands of pamphlets, and without a lawyer in court, became one woman against the United States government. People began to listen to Margaret. She traveled to other countries to teach about birth control, and became the first president of Planned Parentood. Margaret Sanger helped change the law and public opinion. She taught women ways to plan when they wanted their children to be born.

Marie Curie was considered the greatest woman scientist of all time; however, she was not allowed to become a member of the important French Academy of Sciences because she was a woman. In 1979, three hundred years after the establishment of this academy, the first woman was elected as a member.

MARIE SKLODOWSKA CURIE (Poland, /France, 1867-1934)

Marie Curie, as a physicist working with her husband, Pierre, discovered two new elements, polonium and radium. She was the first person to receive two Nobel Prizes.

Marie's father, a professor of physics, encouraged his children's interest in science. Marie worked for five years, saving money to pay for her sister's education in medical school and her own university education. Born and raised in Poland, she moved to Paris, France, graduating as the top student in math and science from the Sorbonne University. Marie was able to combine her career with marriage to scientist Pierre Curie and motherhood. For her doctorate, she studied uranium, noticing strange rays which Marie named "radioactivity." Pierre joined her research, both doing hundreds of tests in the cold uncomfortable shed which was their laboratory, burning their fingers, and exhausting themselves. Because of the many discoveries Marie and Pierre made about radioactivity, they received the Nobel Prize in physics. They found two new elements, "radium" and "polonium" which Marie named for her native country of Poland. Dr. Marie Curie became the first person to receive a second Nobel Prize, this time in chemistry for her work with radium. Because radium burns anything it touches, the Curies thought it might be used to destroy cancer cells. Marie raised money in the U.S. and Europe to buy radium, setting up radium research centers. She never accepted money for her discoveries.

Inspired by Marie Curie, Lise Meitner of Austria wanted to become a physicist. Her loving father, an attorney, warned Lise that only fourteen doctorates had been awarded to women at the University of Vienna since 1365 and none in physics. Lise Meitner was determined, and became the first woman to receive a doctorate in physics from the University of Vienna.

LISE MEITNER (Austria, Germany, Sweden, England, 1878-1968)

Lise Meitner, a nuclear scientist, was the first person to understand that the atom could be split to create tremendous energy.

Lise knew that women in Austria were hardly ever accepted into universities, yet because she was determined to be a scientist, she became the first woman to graduate with a doctoral degree in physics from the University of Vienna. To be near many scientists, she moved to Berlin, Germany, and joined Dr. Otto Hahn in learning more about one of the smallest things in the world, the atom. They worked together for thirty years, discovering a new element called protactinium. Life became unsafe for Lise because the Nazi rulers of Germany were evil to Jewish people and Lise was Jewish. She sadly left her friends and became a citizen of Sweden working in the Nobel Physics Institute. Dr. Otto Hahn wrote Lise asking her to explain a strange reaction he noticed in experiments with uranium atoms. Many important physicists had said that energy hidden in the nucleus (center) of the atom could not be released. Lise suddenly understood this was wrong; the atom could be split which would release 200 million electron volts of energy! Dr. Lise Meitner and her nephew, Dr. Otto Frisch, announced Lise's discovery of "nuclear fission" to the world. Some people used this new discovery in war, creating the atom bomb. Lise hoped atomic energy would be used for peaceful purposes.

15

DIXIE LEE RAY (U.S.A., 1914 -   )

Dixie Lee Ray's career is greatly varied: scientist, politician, working as a marine biologist, chairperson of the Atomic Energy Commission and governor of the state of Washington.

A class in zoology became so interesting to Dixie Lee Ray that she supported herself in all kinds of jobs, including being a janitor, in order to get her doctorate in marine biology from Stanford University. She helped people learn about science by teaching and creating a series of television programs about sea animals. Dixie Lee Ray was asked to be the director of the Pacific Science Center in Seattle, Washington, and later chief scientist on a research ship in the Indian Ocean. Although she was an expert in marine biology, her organizational skills led her to become chairperson of the Atomic Energy Commission. She moved from Washington state to Washington, D.C., and continued to live in her trailer, enjoying simple living and concentrating on work. Dixie Lee Ray brought changes to the Atomic Energy Commission: she created a Department of Safety for the use of nuclear power and helped educate the public about peaceful uses of nuclear power. She was not afraid to speak honestly about problems she saw in the government. Dr. Dixie Lee Ray was able to understand a problem, find a solution and make a decision. She decided to run for the position of governor of the state of Washington. Voters listened to her honesty and elected her the first woman governor of Washington in 1976.

CHIEN SHIUNG WU (China, U.S.A., 1912-   )

Dr. Chien Shiung Wu is thought to be one of the world's best experimental and nuclear physicists.

Chien Shiung Wu's father, a school principal, wanted his daughter to have just as good an education as his sons and encouraged her to study science. She loved math, science and especially physics and graduated from National Central University, Nanking. China was having political problems at the same time that Chien Shiung wanted to continue her studies in the United States. Her parents agreed that she could get her doctorate at the University of California at Berkeley. There she met and married another physics student, and they had one son. Chien Shiung was happiest doing experiments in her laboratory, working as a professor/researcher at Smith College and Princeton and Columbia Universities. During World War II she was asked to work on the secret "Manhattan Project," to create the atomic bomb. Later two physicists had an idea or theory and asked for Dr. Chien Shiung Wu's help. She thought of a way to prove this theory and patiently performed hundreds of experiments. Her findings helped to disprove an important law of physics. The two physicists, the men who had the idea, received the Nobel Prize. Dr. Wu, who did all the experiments, was ignored by the Nobel Committee. She later received many other honors for her work as an experimental physicist.

In the 1800's, most women in Europe and the United States were not allowed to enter universities. Women's colleges in the U.S. were finally created in the middle of the century and some state universities, needing tuition money, also began to accept women. Graduate schools, giving more specialized training, again excluded women. Only very exceptional women were accepted and few became researchers. Florence Sabin was one of the exceptional few.

FLORENCE SABIN (U.S.A., 1871-1953)

One of the greatest women research scientists, Florence Sabin had three careers: teaching future doctors at Johns Hopkins University, researching as a scientist at the Rockefeller Institute for Medical Research, and heading and reforming the Colorado Health Department.

Photo courtesy of Colorado Department of Public Health. A bronze sculpture of Florence Sabin by Joy Buba in the Capitol building, Statuary Hall, Washington, D.C.

On Florence Sabin's seventh birthday, her mother died. As her father could no longer give her a home, she and her sister lived in boarding schools and with relatives. Florence wanted to become a doctor, a career her father had wanted for himself but never achieved. She taught school for two years to pay for her medical school training. While still a medical student, using a microscope and slides, Florence made discoveries about the human lymph system which helped doctors better understand the body. Florence achieved many "firsts" for a woman: first woman professor at Johns Hopkins Medical School and researcher at the Rockefeller Institute; first woman elected president of the American Association of Anatomists; and first woman awarded membership in the National Academy of Sciences. She retired to her home state of Colorado, but not to rest. From the age of seventy-three to eighty, Florence accepted the governor's challenge to improve the health of Colorado's people. New laws, the "Sabin Health Bills," were passed because of Dr. Florence Sabin's hard work. Each state in the U.S. has selected two citizens who best represent their state, and a statue of them is in Washington, D.C., Statuary Hall in the Capitol. Colorado selected Dr. Florence Sabin.

GERTRUDE BELLE ELION (U.S.A., 1918-   )

Gertrude Belle Elion, a research scientist, became the first woman in the National Inventors Hall of Fame, with more than forty-five patents of new drugs bearing her name.

When Gertrude's dearly loved grandfather died of cancer, she made a decision to try to fight this disease through her choice of a career in chemistry. She found scientific research fun and exciting, feeling like a detective working on a mystery. Gertrude did not want to give up the research job she loved to take the time to get a doctorate. Instead she wrote more than 280 scientific papers on her drug discoveries. For over thirty years, working with Dr. George H. Hitchings at the Burroughs Wellcome Company, Gertrude discovered and developed drugs important in fighting leukemia, herpes, malaria, AIDS, and gout, as well as drugs which help in organ transplants. In 1988, Gertrude Elion and George Hitchings won the Nobel Prize in medicine for their work in drug development. They were praised by the Nobel Committee for introducing a clear and orderly way of designing drugs. Gertrude helped create drugs that attacked only certain disease causing cells, not harming the normal cells. In 1991, at the age of seventy-three, Gertrude Belle Elion was the first woman to be invited into the National Inventors Hall of Fame. More than forty-five patents bear the name of this woman who discovered drugs which help people live longer and healthier lives.

BARBARA McCLINTOCK (U.S.A., 1902-1992)

Dr. Barbara McClintock was the first woman to win an unshared Nobel Prize for medicine. Nobel officials called her work "the second great discovery of our time in genetics." As a research doctor in genetics, she discovered "jumping genes."

In high school, Barbara loved science and insisted on going to college. She chose never to marry in order to concentrate on her research as a genetic scientist. She joyfully worked alone for over sixty years. Genes, from the word genetics, are units which cause all living things to be different from each other, such as sizes of people and eye or hair color. Barbara grew colorful corn, called maize, and studied it under the microscope. She noticed something no other scientist had seen before: the genes did not stay in one place, but jumped. Barbara took thousands of careful notes on what she observed. She tried to explain her findings, which were totally different from the ideas of her time. Other scientists refused to accept what she was saying and ignored her. Thirty years later, helped by powerful new microscopes, scientists suddenly understood what Dr. Barbara McClintock had been saying. Barbara's discoveries explained how new species could arise, why cells sometimes change causing cancer and how stress can cause the genes to jump. In her 80s Dr. Barbara McClintock was finally awarded many prizes for her revolutionary work, including the Nobel Prize for Medicine in 1983. Barbara had known her findings were important; she never stopped believing in herself.

GRACE MURRAY HOPPER (U.S.A., 1906-1992)

Grace Murray Hopper created the basis of computer software when she became one of the first computer programmers. She developed her idea of a computer language in English called "COBOL" so that business people and scientists could more easily use computers. She established the entire computer system for the U.S. Navy and became its first woman admiral.

One day, the Mark I computer stopped working and no one could find the cause. Dr. Hopper solved the problem when she found a moth lodged in the computer. She pulled it out with a tweezer and said "There's a bug in it." The word "bug" is still used to describe a computer problem.

From her mother, Grace learned the fun of mathematics. She learned that if one wants to, one can overcome problems as she saw the brave example of her father whose legs had been amputated due to illness. Grace graduated from Vassar College where she later taught mathematics. She then got her doctorate from Yale University. During World War II, Grace joined the U.S. Navy and was assigned to Harvard University, where the first working computer, the Mark I, was being built. Grace was the third person to program this first computer, which was fifty-one feet long. Grace wanted people who were not mathematicians and scientists to be able to use computers. She thought computer language should be in English, but no one agreed with her. For three years, she tried to convince people of this. Her idea was finally accepted and Dr. Grace Murray Hopper helped develop the first English computer language called "COBOL," still used today. The saddest day of Grace's life was when the U.S. Navy asked her to retire at age sixty. Six months later she was asked to come back for temporary duty which lasted twenty years! For her giant strides in changing the way the Navy used computers, Dr. Grace Murray Hopper became the first woman in the history of the U.S. Navy to be appointed admiral.

Some people are very aware of the need to protect our world for future generations. The scientists described in the following pages of this book have shown concern and leadership in paving a new way to cherish life.

RACHEL CARSON (U.S.A., 1907-1964)

Rachel Carson had a reverence for life. Her book <u>Silent Spring</u> changed the way people treated the world, teaching the dangers of using pesticides.

As a child, Rachel saw the beauty in nature, spending time alone near streams and in the woods. At Johns Hopkins University she continued her study of nature through classes in biology (study of life) and zoology (study of animals.) Rachel became head of her family when her sister died, taking care of her mother and two young nieces. She supported them as a biologist at the Bureau of Fisheries in Washington, D.C., writing pamphlets for the government. She also wrote three books about the sea which were so beautifully written that they won many awards. Rachel found out that the government and large companies were spraying pesticides (pest killers) which spread diseases and killed farmers' crops. She learned that more than insects were killed. Birds, butterflies, and fish which ate the pesticides were also beginning to die. People who ate the sprayed plants or fish were becoming sick. Bodies of water and soils were becoming poisoned. Rachel Carson, using her scientific knowledge and talent in writing, carefully gathered facts and wrote the book <u>Silent Spring</u> in 1962. People heard Rachel's warning. Her book was translated into many languages, and governments all over the world changed their laws to protect life.

ELLEN SWALLOW RICHARDS (U.S.A., 1842-1911)

**Ellen Swallow Richards founded two new areas of science:
"ecology," the study of how all living things in the world affect each other
and
"euthenics," based on the idea that improvements in the physical world
lead to improvements in the quality of human life.**

Ellen's earnings as a tutor paid for her university education. She was in the first graduating class of the only college that would accept women, Vassar. Ellen became interested in chemistry and only because her Vassar teachers told the Massachusetts Institute of Technology (MIT) how intelligent Ellen was, did they decide to accept Ellen as their first woman student. MIT would not, however, let her enter the doctoral program because she was a woman, but did give her the unpaid job of training future women scientists. While still a student, she met Robert Richards, one of her professors, whom she later married. As a chemist, she noticed that all living things were affected by air, water, food and soil, and that people became sick if these were not clean. Ellen wanted to awaken three groups: government, industry and the public. She wrote books, lectured, and taught people to <u>demand</u> that their cities give them clean air, water, and food by creating laws to ensure this. She improved the way science was taught in U.S. schools, hoping people would learn not to waste. Ellen Richards created and named two new fields of science: "ecology," how all living things are affected by each other and the world around them, and "euthenics," improving human life by improving the physical world.

ALICE HAMILTON (U.S.A., 1869-1970)

Dr. Alice Hamilton was a pioneer of industrial medicine, helping make the workplaces safer and crusading for laws to protect health.

For twenty-two years Alice chose to live with and be the doctor for the poor people who lived in Chicago's Hull House. Alice noticed that many of the people working in the steel mills, factories and stockyards became very sick because of conditions at their workplace. There were no laws to protect the workers. Dr. Alice Hamilton began to speak about the problems she saw and was appointed by the governor of Illinois to be director of the Occupational Disease Commission. She studied hospital records of factory workers, inspected factories, and spoke to labor leaders and doctors. She found out that many workers were being poisoned by the air in the factories. The air was full of lead dust in paint and lead factories, phosphorus in companies that made matches, and acids in industries that made explosives. People were working in dark, crowded, dusty, unsafe places. Dr. Alice Hamilton wrote many articles and gave speeches warning people of the dangers of industrial poisons. She made the U.S. government aware that laws were needed to protect the workers' health until finally all states had these laws. Dr. Alice Hamilton became the first woman professor at Harvard Medical School, teaching the new area of medicine she had helped create, industrial medicine.

JOY ADAMSON (Austria, Kenya, 1910-1980)

Joy Adamson worked for better understanding of wild animals, helping to keep them free.

Friederike Gessner was nicknamed Joy by her second husband who encouraged her artistic talents. She painted wildfowers and years later preserved on canvas the colorfully dressed people of twenty different African tribes. Her third husband, George Adamson, worked for the Kenya government in Africa, caring for wild animals. One day, to save his life from a charging lion, George shot and killed the beast. He then saw three cubs the mother lion was protecting. Two were given to zoos and the weakest, Elsa, was raised by Joy. George and Joy took daily walks with Elsa, were nuzzled and licked by Elsa, and watched Elsa's family grow. Joy took hundreds of photographs of Elsa and wrote a book about Elsa called <u>Born Free</u>. Because no one had ever lived with lions and returned them to successful lives in the wild, the book became very popular and a movie was made. Joy took most of the profits from her book to form "The Elsa Fund," used to help wild animals remain free. Joy Adamson wrote more books and lectured about her life in Africa with lions, cheetahs, and leopards, helping people better understand wild animals. Tragically, at age seventy Joy was killed, not by a lion but by a man. Joy Adamson had been happiest with the animals of the wild; she had tried to keep them free.

JANE GOODALL (England, Tanzania, 1935-   )

Jane Goodall has lived with and studied chimpanzees in Africa for over thirty years, teaching others to treat with respect this animal so similar to humans.

As a child, Jane was happy for hours in her garden, watching and taking notes about the way birds, insects, and other animals behaved. At age twenty-six, wanting to learn more about animals, Jane got a research job with Dr. Louis Leakey, a famous anthropologist in Africa. Dr. Leakey wanted Jane to study chimpanzees by living near them, watching them, and writing about their habits. Jane moved into the forest and sat quietly during the day watching and learning about chimpanzees. Each night, she wrote everything she had noticed. Jane left Tanzania a few months each year, taking classes at Cambridge University in England to become a Doctor of Primatology (the study of primates which are mammals, such as humans.) She married the man who came to photograph chimpanzees and they raised one child. Jane Goodall loved her study of chimpanzees so much that she spent the next THIRTY YEARS living with and learning about them, writing books and lecturing about her findings. She believes scientific experiments which keep chimpanzees alone for years in cages are very cruel. Dr. Jane Goodall is helping governments, scientists, and zoo keepers treat chimpanzees better both mentally and physically. Chimpanzees are intelligent and social beings with a remarkably similar genetic make-up to human beings.

MARY LEAKEY (England, Tanzania, 1913-   )

Mary Leakey, an archaeologist, led the expedition that found the oldest footprints of our ancestors, proving they walked upright three and one half million years ago.

As a teenager, Mary rebelled against formal schooling. She preferred to attend lectures on a subject often discussed in her home: archaeology, the study of history by finding ancient buried objects. She volunteered to go on excavations to dig into the earth for clues to the past. When stone tools of early people were found, Mary drew them so well she was asked to illustrate a book about archaeology. Dr. Louis Leakey, famous archaeologist, liked Mary's drawings and asked her to illustrate his book. They later married and worked together in Africa, searching for answers to human beginnings found in stone tools and fossils. Fossils are ancient animals or plants that have become hardened into rock. One day Mary's curiosity, patience and training helped her see a small piece of ancient skull on the ground. She carefully dug out the remaining parts, put them together like a puzzle, and found that she had discovered an extinct relative of humans. Several years later, Mary Leakey's expedition found a trail of fossil footprints which looked like footprints of humans walking on two feet. Mary Leakey shocked people by finding proof in stone that human ancestors walked upright at a much earlier date than anyone had thought possible: three and one half million years ago.

MARGARET MEAD (U.S.A., 1901-1978)

Margaret Mead was one of the first anthropologists to study the roles of women and children in different cultures throughout the world. She helped people understand that women and men act in certain ways because their society expects this of them.

Two teachers, Ruth Benedict and Franz Boaz, encouraged Margaret to enter their field of work, anthropology, which is the study of people in different cultures. Dr. Boaz suggested Margaret go far away to Samoa in the Pacific Ocean to learn about the daily life of people on these islands. Margaret sat quietly for hours, carefully noticing people's actions, words and body language. She asked many questions and took notes on all she saw and heard. On one island, she found women were in charge of business and men were creative artists. She began to understand that women and men were not born to behave in certain ways, but often acted in the way their society expected. Margaret made fourteen other trips to study different people. By learning about many cultures she better understood our own values, and taught the public about these values. While working for the American Museum of Natural History and teaching at universities, Dr. Margaret Mead wrote thirty-nine books and thousands of articles, made films and videotapes, and gave hundreds of lectures. She married three times, became the mother of a daughter, and was able to keep friendships with hundreds of people. Margaret Mead taught that while society limits expectations, people can do anything their talents allow.

KAREN HORNEY (Germany, U.S.A., 1885-1952)

Dr. Karen Horney was one of the first psychoanalysts to show the importance of mothering in a person's emotional development, using caring "maternal" support with her patients. She encouraged people to take responsibility for their own actions and to become what she called "self-realized" or truly be themselves.

By age thirteen, Karen knew she wanted to become a doctor. Karen combined marriage and raising three daughters with her career as a psychiatrist. She helped her patients to better understand themselves. Dr. Karen Horney lived in Germany at the time Dr. Sigmund Freud, the famous psychiatrist, said that fathers were the most important parent in forming a child's self-image. Knowing her own mother's great encouragement to her, Dr. Karen Horney had the courage to state a very different opinion: mothers were equally important. Unlike many psychoanalysts, Karen was caring and motherly in dealing with patients, which made them feel comfortable in sharing their thoughts and feelings with her. Karen lectured and wrote six books, all in clear, easy-to-understand language. She wrote in German and later in English, after she moved to the United States in her fifties. She became friends with anthropologist Margaret Mead, sociologist Eric Fromm, and theologist Paul Tillich, and was able to blend what she learned from them to create new ideas. Dr. Karen Horney taught her patients and other psychiatrists that even though our parents are important, we are living today and not in the past. We are responsible for our own actions and can help ourselves.

29

ELISABETH KÜBLER-ROSS (Switzerland, U.S.A., 1926-   )

Elisabeth Kübler-Ross taught people how to face their fear of death so that they could better know how to live. She defined the five stages of grief which help people to better understand themselves and others. She brought the idea of hospice care to the United States.

Elisabeth, born a triplet, was the most independent of the three sisters. As a teenager she left her comfortable home in Switzerland and volunteered to help the people of eastern Europe rebuild their lives after the war. Elisabeth later worked, saving money for medical school training. After her marriage to an American medical student, she moved to the U.S. and became a psychiatrist, helping patients with emotional problems. In the medical schools of the universities of Colorado and Chicago, she had the courage to teach a subject most people do not want to discuss: *death*. She taught that by facing our fears of death, we can live each day more fully. She helped doctors, nurses and clergy understand how a dying person wants to be treated by asking dying people to volunteer to be "teachers." Through the nine books Elisabeth wrote about dying and the world-wide lectures she gave, she helped people understand death and the five stages of grief people experience: denial, anger, bargaining, depression, and acceptance. She wanted very ill people to be able to die in a comfortable home-like place called a hospice, rather than a hospital. She helped set up hospices in many U.S. cities. Dr. Elisabeth Kübler-Ross helped people accept death as a natural part of life.

In our continuing efforts to understand our world, many new areas of science are being studied in the 20th century, from the mysteries of the depths of the oceans to the soaring heights of outer space.

SYLVIA EARLE (U.S.A., 1935-   )

Sylvia Earle has added to our understanding of life beneath the sea through her work as a botanist and aquanaut.

Sylvia grew up on a small farm, encouraged by her mother to see the wonder of snakes, frogs, and plants. By age five, Sylvia knew that she wanted to study animals and plants all her life. She received her doctorate in marine botany (the study of underwater plants) and was a researcher at Harvard University. Sylvia wanted to explore the deep frontier of the ocean. She has spent 6,000 hours diving beneath the seas of the world in her work for government, universities and scientific groups. A few times she was close to sharks. In 1979, Dr. Sylvia Earle set a deep diving record by daring to go down 1,250 feet at 100 feet per minute in a small submarine. Water pressure is greater the deeper one dives. At 600 pounds of pressure per square inch, a leak in the diving suit could have crushed her to death. Dr. Earle was the chief scientist and aquanaut in the underwater laboratory Hydrolab (hydro means water), leading a team of five women scientists who lived underwater for two weeks. Dr. Sylvia Earle is worried about the problem of ocean pollution and thinks that the sea is like a great wilderness which should be explored to help humans survive. She has written articles and books, made speeches, and worked on a television program to teach respect for the ocean frontier we could lose.

SALLY RIDE (U.S.A., 1951-   )

In 1983, Sally Ride became the first United States woman astronaut to orbit the earth in space.

Sally studied math and science in high school and physics, (the study of the laws of nature and the universe) at Stanford University. Sally never dreamed of becoming an astronaut until she saw an ad in the school newspaper by the National Aeronautics Space Administration (NASA) searching for future astronauts. Sally applied, was accepted, and after hundreds of hours of practice, was ready for her first space flight. Airplanes fly six miles above the earth; the spaceship orbits at 200 miles above the earth, traveling at five miles per second. Because there is no gravity in space, astronauts experience being weightless. Sally could float around the space capsule, never using a ladder, moving from one room of the shuttle to another. Even upside down, Sally could still swallow and digest food. She became an inch taller because her spine was not compressed. Drinking glasses are not used because when tipped, a weightless liquid such as milk would stay in the glass; astronauts use straws. Salt shakers are not used as grains of salt would float around the cabin; liquid salt is squeezed into the food cartons instead. Dr. Sally Ride performed many experiments, helping people better understand how life can adapt in space.

In each century there have been a few women who have had the interest, vision and determination to become scientists. Some were encouraged by men; most others, on their own, overcame the barriers of society, became role models, and opened the doors of science for women. Today a small percentage of women work in all areas of science. Girls are often discouraged by parents and teachers at every level. Women with careers in science become discouraged when employers do not promote them merely because they are female. To invite more girls to enter science, parents and teachers must encourage natural curiosity, problem-solving skills, and truly believe that women should have careers in science.

Each invention and discovery is built upon the ideas of others. We need the talents of everyone, female and male, to make our world an even better place. The scientists written about in this book believed in their ideas even when many other people did not. If no one else gives you the encouragement you need to enter the exciting world of science, accept the challenge, and believe in yourself.

Most people can only think of the names of one or two women scientists. The author of this book has compiled names of some award winning as well as ignored scientists of the western world to show the wide variety of scientific work women have accomplished despite the many barriers that were in their paths. Each century, more women scientists added to the improvement of lives. Only a few scientists are listed in the 20th century as history is still being made and many others were not included due to size limitations of this book. The names and deeds of women scientists will continue to grow when societies allow the talents of us all to flourish.

BEFORE 1600s

Merit Ptah	2700 B.C.	Egypt	Earliest known woman doctor
Agamede	12th century B.C.	Greece	Physician; knew much about plants for healing
Agnodike aka Agnodice	4th century B.C.	Greece	Physician who disguised herself as a man to study medicine and work as a doctor because slaves and women were not allowed to practice medicine in Athens
Theano	c.500 B.C.	Greece	Wrote treatises (important papers) about mathematics, physics, and medicine
Arete	fl. 370-340 B.C.	Greece	Head of Cyrenaic School; taught natural science and ethics
Maria the Jewess aka Maria the Prophetess	1st century A.D.	Egypt	Wrote treatises on ancient alchemy; invented laboratory tools to study metals
Olympias	1st century A.D.	Rome	Wrote a book of prescriptions and women's diseases
Aspasia	2nd century A.D.	Rome	Physician, taught importance of preventive medicine during pregnancy; specialized in obstetrics, gynecology, and surgery
Radegund	518-587	Germany	Queen who studied medicine and turned her palace into a hospital
Etheldreda	ca.630-679	England	Abbess who practiced and taught medicine to nuns
Walpurgis	710-778	England	Abbess who studied medicine to help the poor
Adelberger/Bertha	8th century	Italy	Physician in guild
Constanza Calenda	1400s	Italy	First woman doctor with a degree; lectured at University of Naples
Trotula Platearius	11th century d.1097	Italy	Gynecologist and obstetrician; wrote first book on women's health care, used for 300 years
Matilda	fl. 1100-1135	England	Queen, wife of Henry I, nursed sick people in two of the free hospitals she founded
Sarah of St. Gilles	fl. 1326	France	Head of large medical school
Abella	14th century	Italy	Taught at medical school in Salerno; wrote about medical ideas
Dorotea Bocchi	14th century/early 15th	Italy	Professor of medicine at University of Bologna
Alessandra Giliani	1307-1326	Italy	Taught at medical school at Bologna; well respected anatomist
Louyse Bourgeois	1563-1636	France	Wrote about women's body and childbirth for midwives

17th CENTURY

Cornaro Piscopia	in 1678	Italy	Received her Ph.D., University of Padua
Madeleine de Scudery	1607-1701	France	Invited into Italian Academy; not accepted in French Academy because she was a woma
Maria Cunitz	1610-1664	Germany	Astronomer; wrote book simplifying Kepler's Tables of planetary motion
Elizabeth of Bohemia	1618-1680	Bohemia	Influenced the thinking of her teacher, Descartes, a philosopher and mathematician
Margaret Cavendish	1623-1673/4	England	Wrote books about natural philosophy

nne Conway	1631-1679	England	Philosopher; Naturalist; one of first to publicly dispute Descartes; she insisted life could move from simple to complex; she led way for concept of evolution
phra Behn	1640-1689	England	Translated Fontenelle's book on science into English
lisabetha Hevelius	1647-1693	Germany	Astronomer; edited and published catalogue of 1,888 stars and their positions; joint work with her husband
Maria Winkelmann Kirch	1670-1720	Germany	Astronomer; discovered a comet; denied official positions just because she was a woman
Maria Eimmart Müller	1676-1707	Germany	Astronomer; sketched 250 phases of the moon
eanne Dumée	fl . 1680	France	Astronomer; wrote about theories of scientists Copernicus and Galileo
ary Wortley Montagu	1689-1762	England	Brought small pox vaccination to England and Europe
artine de Beausoleil	1600s	France	Considered to be the first woman geologist; studied ore deposits and minerals

18th CENTURY

atherine Bethlen	1700-1759	Hungary	Author of books about science
milie du Châtelet	1706-1749	France	Mathematician; Astronomer; became member of Italian Academy; translated works of Newton and Leibnitz into French; wrote book about physical sciences
aura Bassi	1711-1788	Italy	Physicist; first woman professor of physics at University of Bologna
orothea Erxleben	1715-1762	Germany	First woman to receive a medical degree in Germany
nna Morandi Manzolini	1716-1842	Italy	First licensed physician in Italy, 1760; Anatomy Professor at University of Bologna
Maria Agnesi	1718-1799	Italy	Mathematician; authored books on mathematics, calculus; was not accepted into French Academy of Sciences because she was a female
Marie Biheron	1719-?	France	Created medically correct wax models of the human body
Marie Thiroux d'Arconville	1720-1805	France	Anatomist; produced one of best illustrations of female skeleton in 1759; wrote about chemistry, medicine and natural history
icole-Reine Lepaute	1723-1788	France	Astronomer; wrote about and figured out times and paths of comets, eclipses, planets; crater on the moon is named for her
liza Lucas Pinckney	1723-1793	U.S.A.	Experimented with crops and helped to develop the indigo plant which was good for the economy of southern U.S.A.
iuseppa Barbapiccola	fl.1731	Italy	Translated René Descartes Principles of Philosophy into Italian
atherine Greene	c.1731-1794	U.S.A.	Invented method for separating cotton from its seed; Eli Whitney, whom she helped, got the patent in his name as women could not apply
ouise Elisabeth du Piéry	1746-?	France	First woman Astronomy professor in Paris; figured astronomical tables
Maria Aimée Lullin	1750-1831	Switzerland	Studied insects, bees, with her husband, Francois Huber
aroline Herschel	1750-1848	Germany	Astronomer; first woman to discover a comet; discovered 8 comets, 3 nebulae, published Catalogue of Stars consisting of 1,500 nebulae and star clusters which she and her brother discovered together
riscilla Bell Wakefield	1751-1832	England	Author of books on insects and botany
enier Michiel	1755-1832	Italy	Wrote treatises on botany
Marie Lavoisier	1758-1836	France	Translated scientific works into French; wrote about and illustrated the experiments she and her husband, chemist Antoine Lavoisier, performed
Marie Louise Lachapelle	1769-1821	France	Midwife; wrote books about women's bodies, gynecology and obstetrics
ane Haldimand Marcet	1769-1853	England	Wrote first book on chemistry for female students
Marie Gillain Boivin	1773-1847	France	Midwife; wrote text book about women's bodies, gynecology and obstetrics
ophie Germain	1776-1831	France	Won grand prize of French Academy of Sciences for her work in number theory and vibratrion of elastic surfaces; one of the developers of mathematical physics; her family hid her candles to stop her from studying at night
Maria Dalle Donne	1776/8-1842	Italy	Physician, Director of Midwives at University of Bologna
Madeleine Basseports	-1780	France	Illustrator of rare plants at Paris Botanical Garden

Name	Dates	Country	Description
Mary Somerville	1780-1872	Scotland/England	Wrote books about mathematics, physics, astronomy, science and geography, receiving many honors and awards
James Stuart Barry (Miranda)	1795-1865	Scotland	Army surgeon; graduated Edinburgh School of Medicine; in order to practice medicine, disguised herself as a man, which was discovered at her death
Mary Anning	1799-1847	England	Discovered dinosaur fossils, ichthysoaur and first complete plesiosaur

19TH CENTURY

Name	Dates	Country	Description
Dorothea Dix	1802-1887	U.S.A.	Improved care of mentally ill in U.S.A.
Ada Byron Lovelace	1815-1852	England	Invented the first computer program; the U.S. Defense Department named its programming language "ADA" for her contributions
Amalie Dietrich	1821-1891	Germany	Naturalist, collected birds, mammals, plants for museums
Elizabeth Agassiz	1822-1907	U.S.A.	Author of books about natural history; popularized her husband, Dr. Louis Agassiz's ideas; first president of Radcliffe College
Emily Blackwell	1826-1910	U.S.A.	Physician; as professor, trained many women to become doctors in women's medical school she founded with her sister, Elizabeth Blackwell
Eleanor Ormerod	1828-1901	England	Considered the first woman professional entomologist, studying and writing about insec
Marianne North	1830-1890	England	Wrote and illustrated books about plants and animals she found on her world travels
Clemence Augustine Royer	1830-1902	France	Translated Charles Darwin's Origin of Species into French
Isabella Bird Bishop	1831-1904	England	Naturalist, Geographer; wrote A Lady's Life in the Rocky Mountains based on her trave
Lucy Hobbs Taylor	1833-1910	U.S.A.	Dentist, first woman to attend and graduate from a dental school in 1866
Rebecca Lee	?	U.S.A.	Physician; first black American woman to receive medical degree from New England Female Medical College in 1864; practiced in Richmond, Virginia
Elizabeth Anderson	1836-1917	England	Physician; helped to open British medical schools to women
Mary Adelaide Nutting	1838-1948	U.S.A.	Wanted university education for nurses
Sophia Jex-Blake	1840-1912	England	Founded London School of Medicine for Women
Linda Richards	1841-1930	U.S.A.	Received first U.S. nursing diploma; opened first nursing school in Japan
Agnes Clerke	1842-1907	Ireland	Astronomer; author of books about astronomy
Mary Putnam Jacoobi	1842-1906	U.S.A.	Physician; helped more women to become doctors
Mary Eliza Mahoney	1845-1926	U.S.A.	Nurse; first black woman to graduate from a professional white nursing school, 1879
Rebecca Cole	1846-1922	U.S.A.	Physician; one of first black women doctors; graduated 1867 from Women's Medical College of Pennsylvania; one of first house call doctors in slum neighborhoods working with Elizabeth Blackwell; helped start Women's Directory to provide medical and legal help to women in Philadelphia
Marie Heim-Vögtlin	1846-1914	Switzerland	Doctor; opened hospital for women and nurse training school in Switzerland
Jane Harrison	1850-1928	England	Archaeologist with new ideas about ancient Greek culture
Sofia Kovalevskaia aka Sonya Kovalévsky	1850-1891	Russia	Won an important prize from the French Academy of Sciences for her work in mathematics; in 1874, received her doctorate in philosophy; became professor at University of Stockholm
Clara Cummings	1853-1906	U.S.A.	Botanist; researched and wrote about mosses in field of lichenology
Hertha Ayrton	1854-1923	England	Physicist; researched electric arc and sand ripples; first woman to read her paper before Royal Society as women were not allowed to do this
Aletta Jacobs	1854-1929	Holland	One of first women physicians in Holland; opened world's first birth control clinic in Amsterdam
Louise Bethune	1856-1913	U.S.A.	First U.S. woman architect
Margaret Maltby	1860-1944	U.S.A.	Physicist; first woman to receive a doctorate from Göttingen University, Germany
Jane Addams	1860-1935	U.S.A.	Created Hull House where immigrants received preventive medicine, job training, legal protection; first woman to receive Nobel Peace Prize

Name	Dates	Country	Description
ttie Stevens	1861-1912	U.S.A.	Biologist; Geneticist; found X and Y chromosomes which determine sex of embryo; Edmund B. Wilson duplicated her findings and got the credit
ı Andreas Salomé	1861-1937	France	One of first female psychotherapists (doctor who treats mental and emotional problems; author
rence Bascom	1862-1945	U.S.A.	Geologist (study of the earth;) first woman to get B.S., M.S., and Ph.D. from Johns Hopkins University; first woman employed by U.S. government as a geologist
rence Bailey	1863-1948	U.S.A.	Naturalist; observed and wrote about birds, study of ornithology
ry Whiton Calkins	1863-1930	U.S.A.	Psychologist; first woman president of American Psychological Association
nie Jump Cannon	1863-1941	U.S.A.	Astronomer; classified 350,000 stars; published 10-volume star catalogue
na Wessel Williams	1863?-1954	U.S.A.	Discovered cause of diptheria, developed antitoxin for it; brought rabies antitoxin to U.S.A. from France
tha Van Hoosen	1863-1952	U.S.A.	Surgeon; founded American Medical Women's Association, 1915; wrote books about female surgeons
th Cavell	1865-1915	England	Nurse, who because she treated all soldiers on both sides of war, was put to death
ury Antonia Pereira	1866-1952	U.S.A.	Astronomer who developed a new way to classify stars
e Campbell Hurd-Mead	1867-1941	U.S.A.	Doctor and medical historian; wrote two books on history of women in medicine
ian Wald	1867-1940	U.S.A.	Nurse; started first public health center in U.S.A. in New York
Gray	1867-1953	U.S.A.	First black female dentist; doctor of dental surgery degree from University of Michigan Dental School, 1890
ilie Snethlage	1868-1929	Germany/Brazil	Zoologist, author; Director of Zoological Museum and Gardens in Brazil
rietta Swan Leavitt	1868-1921	U.S.A.	Astronomer whose discoveries about variable stars later made it possible for Edwin Hubble to show that our galaxy is only one of billions in universe
er Pohl Lovejoy	1870-1967	U.S.A.	Physician; director, organizer Women's Hospital Service; wrote book about women doctors
garet Floy Washburn	1871-1939	U.S.A.	Psychologist; wrote textbook on comparative psychology and co-editor "American Journal of Psychology"
a Morgan	1872-1957	U.S.A.	Architect; Civil Engineer; designed one of largest and most unusual homes in U.S., San Simeon in California
y Swartz Rose	1874-1941	U.S.A.	First professor of nutrition in U.S. in 1921; first to use serving size and recipe amounts
othy Mendenhall	1875-1964	U.S.A.	Physician; discovered the cell which causes Hodgkins disease
an Gilbreth	1878-1972	U.S.A.	Industrial engineer, management consultant; founded field of scientific study of time saving ideas
a Roberts	1879-1965	U.S.A.	Headed committee that first listed suggestions of which foods people should ideally eat each day, "Recommended Daily Nutrition Guide"
ie Stopes	1880-1958	England	Founded England's first family planning center
ıy Noether	1882-1935	Germany	Mathematical genius, considered best woman mathematician ever to have lived; worked out mathematical problems which helped physicists use Einstein's theory of relativity; made major contributions in algebra
cis Reed Elliot Davis	1882-1964	U.S.A.	First black nurse in American Red Cross
nie Klein	1882-1960	Austria/England	Psychoanalyst; emhasized the infant within the child
ne Deutsch	1884-1982	Germany/USA	Psychonalyst; wrote controverial books about psychology of women
se Pearce	1835/6-1959	U.S.A.	Pathologist; co-inventor of serum that cures sleeping sickness
ıbeth Hazen	1885-1975	U.S.A.	Microbiologist; worked with Rachel Fuller Brown and together they developed Nystatin, powerful drug used against human fungus infections
Hollingworth	1886-1939	U.S.A.	Pioneer in clinical psychology and education of exceptional children
Benedict	1887-1948	U.S.A.	Anthropologist; author; studied Japanese culture
ie Hyman	1888-1969	U.S.A.	Zoologist; wrote complete book about animals without backbones; had 3 Ph.d.s.
Deloria	1889-1971	U.S.A.	Anthropologist; as a Dakota Indian, wrote books about her tribe's language and customs
Caldwell	1890-1972	U.S.A.	Chemistry professor; developed method of isolating enzymes to easily study them
a Quimby	1891-1982	U.S.A.	Began the field of Radiation Physics, finding how to measure exact radiation amounts for each patient

Martha May Eliot	1891-1978	U.S.A.	Co-developer of cure for rickets
Clara Thompson	1893-1958	U.S.A.	Psychiatrist, Psychoanalyst; wrote book explaining psychology of women
Cicely Williams	1893-?	Jamaica/England	Pediatrician (children's doctor) in Ghana, Africa; black doctor, she found cause of disease Kwashiorkor occurs when starving people do not get enough protein
Anna Freud	1895-1982	Germany/England	Used her knowledge of psychoanalytic ideas to help children, pioneering this field
Wanda Kirkbridge Farr	1895-	U.S.A.	Cytologist; studied plant cell membranes to find structure of cellulose; one of first to use X-Rays to analyze fibers
Rebecca Lancefield	1895-1981	U.S.A.	Bacteriologist; first to find organism which causes rheumatic fever
May E. Chinn	c.1896-1980	U.S.A.	Doctor; graduated Bellevue Medical Center; father had been a slave; mother scrubbed floors to help pay for May's education
Gerty Theresa Cori	1896-1957	Czech/U.S.A.	First U.S. woman to receive Nobel Prize, shared with her husband in Medicine and Physiology; they made discoveries on how the body uses sugar and starch (the metabolism of carboyhydrates and how glycogen is changed to glucose)
Ida Noddack	1896-1978	Germany	Discoverer of element rhenium
Irène Joliet-Curie	1897-1956	France	Shared the Nobel Prize in Chemistry with her husband for discovery of artificial radioactive isotopes; she was the daughter of Marie Curie; they are the only mother and daughter to have won Nobel Prizes
Mary Engle Pennington	1897-1952	U.S.A.	Bacteriological Chemist; research led to development of frozen foods; first chief of U.S. Research Food Laboratory
Helen Brooke Taussig	1898-1986	U.S.A.	Physician, Surgeon; saved lives of "blue babies" with her idea of operating on blood vessels near the heart; first physician to warn of dangers of thalidomide, medicine which caused malformed babies; first woman elected president of American Heart Association
Katherine Burr Blodgett	1898-1979	U.S.A.	Research Physicist; Chemist; invented non-reflecting glass
Rachel Fuller Brown	1898-1980	U.S.A.	Microbioloist; worked with Elizabeth Hazen to develop drug, Nystatin
Margaret A. Boas Fixsen	1899-	?	Her research led to discovery of vitamin Biotin or vitamin H

..... SOME ..... WOMEN SCIENTISTS OF THE 20TH CENTURY

Hattie Alexander	1901-1968	U.S.A.	Bacteriologist; discovered cure for bacterial meningitis
Dorothy Hansine Anderson	1901-	?	First to identify and find easy way to diagnose cystic fibrosis
Mina Rees	1902-	U.S.A.	First woman president of American Association for the Advancement of Science
Irmgard Flugge Lotz	1903-1974	Germany	Aeronautical engineer; researcher; helped develop first automatic aircraft controls
Gladys Anderson Emerson	1903-	U.S.A.	First to isolate and study Vitamin E
Ruth Ella Moore	1903-	U.S.A.	First black woman Ph.D. in Bacteriology
Helen Sawyer Hogg	1905-	U.S.A./Canada	Astronomy professor, University of Toronto; wrote books on variable stars; discovered 99 of the 329 variable stars known
Rosita Rivera Ramirez	1906-	Philippine Islands	Doctor; established a hospital and nursing school in Philippines
Maria Goeppert Mayer	1906-1972	Poland/U.S.A.	Shared Nobel Prize in Physics for researching atomic nuclei
Ruth Patrick	1907-	U.S.A.	Ecologist; Limnologist; invented diatometer which measured pollution in water
Virginia Apgar	1909-1974	U.S.A.	Anesthesiologist; invented test for new babies to immediately find out baby's physical condition
Mary Steichen Calderone	1909-	U.S.A.	Gynecologist; founded Sex Information and Education Council of U.S., 1964
Rita Levi-Montalcini	1909-	Italy	Neurobiologist; made discoveries of brain nerve connections and co-discoverer of Nerve Growth Factor; received joint Nobel Prize, Physiology and Medicine, 1986
Marguerite Perey	1909-1975	France	Nuclear Chemist; discovered francium, a radioactive element
Dorothy Crowfoot Hodgkin	1910-	England	Chemist; received Nobel Prize for Chemistry, 1964; discovered chemical structure of penicillin and vitamin B-12

ladys Hobby	1910-	U.S.A.	Microbiologist, with a team produced the first usable penicillin; developed terramycin antibiotic
orothy Horstman	1911-	U.S.A.	Doctor who identified polio virus in early stages
attie Alexander	1911-1968	U.S.A.	Bacteriologist; discovered cure for bacterial meningitis
lizabeth Shull Russell	1913-	U.S.A.	Zoologist, Geneticist; discovered gene which causes muscular distrophy
rances Kelsey	1914-	U.S.A.	Pharmacologist; working for Food and Drug Administration, refused to approve drug, thalidomide, saving many U.S. children from birth defects
stelle Ramey	1917-	U.S.A.	Physiologist; Endocrinologist; wrote 150 research papers on endocrinology; second president of Association for Women in Science (AWIS)
ne C. Wright	1919-	U.S.A.	Pioneer work in cancer chemotherapy; first black woman to be appointed to a high post in medical administration
osalind Franklin	1920-1958	England	Biophysicist; described DNA molecule which helped J.D. Watson and F.H. Crick make a DNA model (DNA helps scientists understand genetic code of body)
osalyn Yalow	1921-	U.S.A.	Shared Nobel Prize in Medicine, 1977, for creation of radioimmunoassay, which is method to exactly measure hormones, vitamins, drugs in body
ugenie Clark	1922-	U.S.A.	Marine Biologist; director and founder of world's largest shark study institute
tephanie Kwolek	1923-	U.S.A.	Research chemist who invented Kevlar, a fiber strong as steel used in space vehicles, planes, radial tires
oanne Simpson	1923-	U.S.A.	First woman to receive degree in Meteorology; Director of National Oceanic and Atmospheric Administration Meteorology Laboratory
ewel Plummer Cobb	1924-	U.S.A.	Biologist; cancer researcher; 1981 became president California State University, Fullerton; one of few African-American women to head a university
arilyn Jacox	1929-	U.S.A.	Intermolecular Biologist; researched structure and chemical reactivity of radical ions
larice D. Reid	1931-	U.S.A.	Physician; because of her black heritage, researched sickle-cell anemia; educated public and developed national programs to reduce deaths from this disease
ian Fossey	1932-1985	U.S.A.	Primatologist; researched and helped preserve African mountain gorilla
alentina Tereshkova	1937-	Russia	Astronaut; first woman in space, June 16,1963
ocelyn Bell Burnell	1943-	England	Radio Astronomer; 1967 first person to notice pulsars which led to discovery of black holes in space
aye Wattleton	1943-	U.S.A.	Nurse; President Planned Parenthood; black woman helping protect all women's right to choose whether and when to have children
irute Galdikas	1947-	Germany/Canada	Primatologist; provided most complete study of orangutan, Indonesia
ae C. Jemison	1956-	U.S.A.	Astronaut; Physician; world's first black female astronaut
llen Ochoa	1959-	U.S.A.	First Hispanic female astronaut

..................to be continued in this century and beyond.

BIBLIOGRAPHY

Abell, George O., Morrison, David, Wolff, Sidney, Exploration of the Universe. Philadelphia; London: Saunders College Publishing, 1991. Harcourt Brace, Jovanovich College Publishers, 1993.

Abram, Ruth J., Ed., Send Us A Lady Physician, Women Doctors in America 1835-1920. New York; London: W.W. Norton & Company, 1985.

Arnold, Lois Barber, Four Lives in Science, Women's Education in the 19th Century. New York: Schocken Books, 1984.

Bateson, Mary Catherine, With A Daughter's Eye: A Memoir of Margaret Mead and Gregory Bateson. New York: Morrow Company, 1984.

Billings, Charlene W., Grace Hopper: Navy Admiral and Computer Pioneer. Hillside, New Jersey: Enslow Publisher, 1989.

Bluemel, Elinor, Florence Sabin: Colorado Woman of the Century. Boulder, Colorado: University of Colorado Press, Johnson Publishing Company, 1959.

Bourdillon, Hilary, Women as Healers: A History of Women and Medicine. Cambridge, England; New York: Cambridge University Press, 1988.

Bolton, Sarah Knowles, Lives of Girls Who Became Famous. New York: Crowell Co., 1949.

Bronowski, Jacob, Common Sense of Science. Cambridge, Massachusetts: Harvard University Press, 1978.

Bronowski, Jacob, Science and Human Values. New York: Harper and Row, 1956.

Brooks, Paul, The House of Life: Rachel Carson at Work. Boston: Houghton Mifflin Company, 1972.

Carwell, Hattie, Blacks in Science: Astrophysicist to Zoologist. New York: Exploration Press, 1977.

Chicago, Judy. The Dinner Party. New York: Anchor Press, Doubleday, 1979.

Clarke Robert, Ellen Swallow: The Woman Who Founded Ecology. Chicago: Follett Publishing Company, 1973.

Crawford, Deborah, Lise Meitner, Atomic Pioneer. New York: Crown Publishers, Inc., 1969.

Curie, Eve, Madame Curie, A Biography. Garden City, New York: Doubleday, Doran Company, 1937.

Current Biography. "Sylvia A. Earle." Volume 53, Number 5, May, 1992, pp. 21-25.

Dash, Joan, The Triumph of Discovery, Women Scientists Who Won the Nobel Prize. Englewood Cliffs, New Jersey: Julian Messner of Simon Schuster, Inc., 1991.

Earle, Sylvia, "Exploring the Deep Frontier." Lecture presented August 3, 1992, The Denver Museum of Natural History.

Gill, Derek, Quest: The Life of Elisabeth Kübler-Ross. New York: Harper and Row, 1980.

Gleasner, Diana C., Breakthrough, Women in Science. New York: Walker and Company, 1983.

Goodall, Jane, Lecture presented at The Denver Museum of Natural History, April 4, 1991.

Greene, Timothy, The Restless Spirit: Profiles in Adventure. New York: Walker and Company, 1970.

Grey, Vivian, Secret of the Mysterious Rays, Discovery of Nuclear Energy. New York: Basic Books, 1966.

Grinstein, Louise and Campbell, Paul, Women of Mathematics. Westport, Connecticut: Greenwood Press, Inc., 1987.

Howard, Jane, Margaret Mead, A Life. New York: Simon Schuster, 1984.

Haber, Louis, Women Pioneers of Science. New York: Harcourt, Brace, Jovanovich, Inc., 1979.

Hellemans, Alexander, Bunch, Bryan, The Timetables of Science, A Chronology of the Most Important People and Events in the History of Science. New York: Simon & Schuster, Inc., 1988.

Holloway, Marguerite, "Profile: Sylvia A. Earle." Scientific American, April, 1991, pp. 37-40.

Holloway, Marguerite, "Profile: Gertrude Belle Elion." Scientific American, October, 1991, pp. 40-44.

Hurd-Mead, Kate Campbell, A History of Women in Medicine. Haddam, Connecticut: The Haddam Press, 1938.

Igus, Toyomi, Ed., Book of Black Heroes, Great Women in the Struggle. New Jersey: Just Us Books, 1991.

Kahle, Jane Butler, Ed., Women in Science, A Report from the Field. Philadelphia: Falmer Press, 1985.

Krucoff,, Carol, "Antonia Novello, A Dream Come True," The Saturday Evening Post. May/June, 1991, pp. 38-41.

Kulkin, Mary Ellen, Her Way: Biographies of Women for Young People. Chicago: American Library Association, 1976.

Latham, Jean Lee, Elizabeth Blackwell, Pioneer Woman Doctor. Champaign, Illinois: Garrard Publishing Company, 1975.

Leakey, Mary D., Disclosing the Past. Garden City, New York: Doubleday, 1984.

Lopate, Carol, Women in Medicine. Baltimore, Maryland: Published for the Josiah Macy, Jr.. Foundation, The Johns Hopkins, Press, 1968

Luria, S.E., Life, The Unfinished Experiment. New York: Scribner, 1973.

Mead, Margaret, Blackberry Winter. New York: William Morrow and Co., 1972.

Morantz-Sanchez, Regina Markell, Sympathy and Science: Women Physicians in American Medicine. New York: Oxford University Press, 1985.

Noble, Iris, Contemporary Women Scientists of America. New York: Julian Messner, 1979.

Opfell, Olga S., The Lady Laureates: Women Who Have Won the Nobel Prize. Metuchen, New Jersey: Scarecrow Press, 1978.

Ogilvie, Marilyn Bailey, Women in Science, Antiquity Through the 19th Century. Cambridge, Massachusettes: MIT Press, 1986.

O'Neill, Louis Decker, Ed., The Women's Book of World Records and Achievments. New York: Anchor Press, Doubleday, 1979.

Phelan, Mary Kay, Probing the Unknown, The Story of Dr. Florence Sabin. New York: Thomas Crowell Co., 1969.

Rubins, Jack, M.D., Karen Horney: Gentle Rebel of Psychoanalysis. New York: Dial Press, 1978.

Sanger, Margaret, My Fight for Birth Control. New York: Farrar and Rinehart, Inc., 1931.

Sayers, Janet, Mothers of Psychoanalysis: Helene Deutch, Karen Horney, Anna Freud, and Melanie Klein. New York: W. W. Norton & Co., 1991.

Schiebinger, Londa, The Mind Has No Sex? Women in the Origins of Modern Science. Cambridge, Massachusettes: Harvard University Press, 1989.

Selye, Hans, From Dream to Discovery, On Being a Scientist. New York: McGraw-Hill, 1964.

Sinderman, Carl J., The Joy of Science. New York: Plenum Press, 1985.

Turner, Dorothy, Florence Nightingale. New York: Bookwright Press, 1986.

Vare, Ethlie Ann and Ptacek, Greg, Mothers of Invention: From the Bra to the Bomb: Forgotten Women and Their Unforgetable Ideas. New York: Morrow, 1988.

Verrengia, Joseph B. "Expert Seeks Chance for Chimps." Rocky Mountain News, March 22, 1991.

Yost, Edna, Women of Modern Science. New York: Dodd, Mead & Comapany, 1960.

Zuckerman, Harriet, Cole, Jonathan R., and Bruer, John T., Ed., The Outer Circle, Women in the Scientific Community. New York: W. W. Norton & Company, Inc., 1991.

**Additional books by Vivian Sheldon Epstein
available by ordering from
your local bookstore, wholesale distributor or
VSE Publisher, 212 South Dexter Street, Denver, Colorado 80222**

A common thread among all these books is the elimination of prejudice and the growth of the individual through knowledge that the world is open to us with many possibilities. Role models of the past are depicted to inspire young people. The author believes that changes in societal attitudes can best be created by instilling positive ideas within the younger child.

HISTORY OF WOMEN ARTISTS FOR CHILDREN

First book ever written for young people ages 5 to 12 telling women's story as artists from the 1500s to the present. Beautiful museum color reproductions. *Booklist* . . . "worthwhile and profusely illustrated" (March 88); *National Art Education Association* . . . "very attractive, interesting and information packed" (October 88). Chosen by *Choices* as one of best books of 1987. 32 pages, 8"x12", 16 in full vibrant color. Soft Cover: ISBN 0-9601002-5-3; $6.95; Hard Cover: ISBN 0-9601002-6-1; $13.95.

HISTORY OF WOMEN FOR CHILDREN

The Council on Interracial Books for Children called this book "EXTRAORDINARY." For the first time, a chronological story of the history of women for children is told; ages 5 to 12. Highlighted as one of five of the best 600 childrens' books in ten years by *A Guide to Non-Sexist Children's Books, Vol. II: 1976-1985.* 32 pages, 8"x12", 8 in full vibrant color. Soft Cover: ISBN 0-9601002-3-7; $5.95; Hard Cover: 0-9601002-4-5; $12.95.

THE ABCS OF WHAT A GIRL CAN BE

Delightful alphabet book describing wide range of professions available to women today, all with non-sexist job titles. Attractive color drawings accompany rhyming text. For pre-school and early elementary. 32 pages, 8"x12", 8 in full vibrant color. Soft cover: ISBN 0-9601002-2-9; $5.95.

Please add $1.50 postage; Colorado residents add sales tax.

COMMENTS ABOUT
HISTORY OF WOMEN IN SCIENCE FOR YOUNG PEOPLE
MADE JUST PRIOR TO PUBLICATION

"Through the thorough research and thoughtful attention to detail, Vivian Sheldon Epstein has compiled an inspirational picture of the role of women in science throughout history. As an attorney and a scientist, I welcome the emergence of such positive and dynamic models for today's young women."

Lynda M. Fox, J.D., Attorney, Clinical Laboratory Specialist in Cytogenetics, with the Eleanor Roosevelt Institute for Cancer Research, home of the Florence R. Sabin Laboratory for Developmental Genetic Medicine, affiliate of the University of Colorado Health Sciences Center, Denver, Colorado

"These biographical vignettes provide inspiration and information regarding female scientists, mathematicians, and doctors. Students in search of female role models in the field of the sciences will be well served by this collective biography."

Pam Sandlian, Denver Public Library Children's Library Manager, Denver, Colorado

"This book will be an outstanding resource for schools to show examples of role models for women in science."

Jack Platt, Ed.D., Director of Curriculum and Program Development for the Cherry Creek School District, Englewood, Colorado

"How refreshing to read material so well researched of history and history in the making. Hopefully, readers will appreciate a work so accurately written which brings to the forefront our great women in science and in the space program. We, at NASA, have always worked with high caliber female and male engineers and scientists of which Sally Ride is one fine example among many."

Angelo M. Nowlin, Aerospace Engineer, National Aeronautical Space Administration (NASA), Advance X-Ray Astrophysics Facility, Huntsville, Alabama

"Often girls are unaware of the opportunities open to them. This book reminds them that courageous women have opened new pathways in science for all of us."

Jane S. Day, Ph.D. Archaeology, Chief Curator of the Denver Museum of Natural History, Denver, Colorado

"Women have been scientists for centuries and their role as discoverers and researchers was never more important than it is today! This timely book reminds us that science is for all people. Women scientists are part of our history and important for our future!"

Anne Tweed, National Science Teachers Association District Director, Science Coordinator and Science Teacher for Eaglecrest High School, Cherry Creek School District, Englewood, Colorado